Brighton

Brighton

Helen Livingstone

Waterton Press Limited

First published in the United Kingdom in 1998 by
Frith Publishing an imprint of Waterton Press Limited.

British Library Cataloguing in Publication Data.

Helen Livingston
Brighton

ISBN 1-84125-010-4

Reproductions of all the photographs in this book are available as framed or mounted prints. For more information please contact The Francis Frith Collection at the address below quoting the title of this book and the page number and photograph number or title.

The Francis Frith Collection,
PO Box 1697, Salisbury, Wilts SP3 5TW
Tel: 01747 855 669
E mail: bookprints@francisfrith.com

Typeset in Bembo Semi Bold

Printed and bound in Great Britain by
WBC Limited, Bridgend, Glamorgan.

Contents

Francis Frith 1822-1898

Introduction

Francis Frith:
A Victorian Pioneer

Francis Frith, the founder of the world famous photographic archive was a complex and multitudinous man. A devout Quaker and a highly successful and respected Victorian businessman he was also a flamboyant character.

By 1855 Frith had already established a wholesale grocery business in Liverpool and sold it for the astonishing sum of £200,000, equivalent of over £15,000,000 today. Now a multi-millionaire he was able to indulge in his irresistible desire to travel. As a child he had poured over books penned by early explorers, and his imagination had been stirred by family holidays to the sublime mountain regions of Wales and Scotland. "What a land of spirit-stirring and enriching scenes and places!" he had written. He was to return to these scenes of grandeur in later years to "recapture the thousands of vivid and tender memories", but with a very different purpose. Now in his thirties, and captivated by the new science of photography, Frith set out on a series of pioneering journeys to the Middle East, that occupied him from 1856 until 1860.

He took with him a specially-designed wicker carriage which acted as camera, dark-room and sleeping chamber. These far-flung journeys were full of intrigue and adventure. In his life story, written when he was sixty-three, Frith tells of being held captive by bandits, and fighting "an awful midnight battle to the very point of exhaustion and surrender with a deadly pack of hungry, wild dogs". He bargained for several weeks with a "mysterious priest" over a beautiful seven-volume illuminated Koran, which is now in the British Museum. Wearing full arab costume, Frith arrived at Akaba by camel seventy years before Lawrence of Arabia, where he encountered "desert princes and rival sheikhs, blazing with jewel-hilted swords".

During these extraordinary adventures he was assiduously exploring the desert regions of the nile and recording the antiquities and people with his camera, Frith was the first photographer ever to travel beyond the sixth cataract. Africa, we must remember, was still the "Dark Continent", and Stanley and Livingstone's famous meeting was a decade into the future. The conditions for picture taking confound belief. He laboured for hours on end in his dark-room in the sweltering heat, while the volatile collodion chemicals fizzed dangerously in their trays. Often he was forced to work in tombs and caves where conditions were cooler.

Back in London he exhibited his photographs and was "rapturously cheered" by the Royal Society. His reputation as a photographer was made overnight. His photographs were issued in albums by James S. Virtue and William MacKenzie, and published simultaneously in London and New York. An eminent historian has likened their impact on the population of the time to that on our own generation of the first photographs taken on the surface of the moon.

Characteristically, Frith spotted the potential to create a new business as a specialist publisher of photographs. In 1860 he married Mary Ann Rosling and set out to photograph every city, town and village in Britain. For the next thirty years Frith travelled the country by train and by pony and trap, producing photographs that were keenly bought by the millions of Victorians who, because of the burgeoning rail network, were beginning to enjoy holidays and day trips to Britain's seaside resorts and beauty spots.

To meet the demand he gathered together a team of up to twelve photographers, and also published the work of independent artist-photographers of the reputation of Roger Fenton and Francis Bedford. Together with clerks and photographic printers he employed a substantial staff at his Reigate studios. To gain an understanding of the scale of Frith's business one only has to look at the catalogue issued by Frith & Co. in 1886. It runs to some 670 pages listing not only many thousands of views of the British Isles but also photographs of most major European countries, and China, Japan, the USA and Canada. By 1890 Frith had created the greatest specialist photographic publishing company in the world.

He died in 1898 at his villa in Cannes, his great project still growing. His sons, Eustace and Cyril, took over the task, and Frith & Co. continued in business for another seventy years, until by 1970 the archive contained over a third of a million pictures of 7,000 cities, towns and villages.

The photographic record he has left to us stands as a living monument to a remarkable and very special man.

Frith's dhow in Egypt *c.*1857

CHAPTER 1
THE PIERS

A walk to the end of the pier has been an essential ingredient in a Brighton holiday since the Chain Pier opened in 1823. This pier was designed as a landing stage for the cross-channel trade (Brighton to Dieppe was on the quickest route between London and Paris), but it was immediately popular with 'promenaders' who paid 2*d* or one guinea annually to walk the 13 ft wide, 1,154 ft long wooden deck. Brighton's Chain Pier was the first pleasure pier ever built, with kiosk's contained in its towers and other attractions, including a camera obscura, at the shore end. The pier stood just to the east of the present Palace Pier, but today nothing remains.In its day it was a particularly fine structure and inspired both Constable and Turner to paint it. Entrance was via a new esplanade along the foot of the cliff, where the Aquarium (now the Sea Life Centre) now stands. The Chain Pier's popularity took a tumble, and in 1891 the Marine Palace and Pier Company was given permission to build a new pier (Palace Pier), on condition that they demolish the Chain Pier. The company did not have to fulfil this condition as it was completely destroyed in a storm on 4th December 1896.

The West Pier, by the famous pier designer, Eugenius Birch, opened in 1866, providing a fashionable promenade pier for the western side of Brighton. Initially there were few buildings on the pier, but in 1893 the pier head was widened and a large pavilion built. This was converted to a theatre in 1903 (it had its own repertory company during the 1930s) but in 1945 it was turned into an amusement arcade. A concert hall was added in the centre in 1916. Day trips to France from the West Pier were very popular during the inter-war years.

The Palace Pier opened in 1899 and was straight away a huge success. In 1901 it was embellished with a landing stage and oriental style pier head pavilion. The pavilion was remodelled as a theatre in 1910-11 at the same time as the bandstand (now the cafes) and the Winter Garden (now the Palace of Fun) were added. The theatre was demolished in 1974 after severe damage by a barge associated with demolition of the landing stage. Pier head slot machines and funfair rides took its place. The Palace Pier has always been extremely popular, rising to its apex in 1939 when 2 million people visited it, 45,000 in just one bank holiday.

48513
The Palace Pier opened in 1899. This 1902 view shows the recently completed oriental pier head pavilion - the Marine Pavilion.

48509
1902 view of the Palace Pier, from the sea, showing the elegant Brighton seafront and several pleasure craft.

B2085017

View of the Chain Pier from the west which shows the pier head, designed as a landing stage for cross-channel traffic.

B208022
This busy summer scene in the 1950s looking east shows the remodelled entrance to the Palace Pier and the eastern beaches.

B208103
Looking east from the Palace Pier in 1955 towards Black Rock, an area now dominated by the concrete break-water of the Brighton Marina.

B208112

This 1960s view of the Palace Pier from Marine Parade shows it developed since 1902, with the addition of an entrance, clocktower and winter gardens.

B2085018

The historic West Pier was opened in 1866. This 1880s view shows the Pier before its extensive additions from 1890 onwards.

33717
An 1894 view shows the West Pier during the 'fashionable' autumnal season, sporting its new pier head pavilion and landing stage.

22345
This 1889 view shows a still undeveloped West Pier. Beached boats are a reminder of Brighton's days as a fishing village.

33762
This 1894 view shows the West Pier, its landing stage and paddle steamers. Benches are visible on the beach – the forerunners of deckchairs.

B2085009
The 1896 storm that destroyed the Chain Pier, badly damaged the West Pier, as this picture shows, and the partly built Palace Pier.

48493
A glorious summer's day in 1902 showing the West Pier beach, busy with holidaymakers, bathing machines and boats.

33718
Another 1894 view of the West Pier, this time looking from the east with horse-drawn conveyances waiting for custom.

48508

There was a thriving trade in excursions along the coast and to France. This 1902 view shows a ferry, probably the *Brighton Queen*, leaving the West Pier.

48494

This 1902 view shows the front of the 1,115 ft West Pier, showing clearly the two toll booths - only the left booth now survives.

48495
Another 1902 view of the West Pier. Note the fishing boats out at sea beyond the left hand toll booth.

48497
Looking back to the shore from the West Pier in 1902. The delicate wrought-iron features of this Victorian masterpiece are clearly visible.

71495

This 1921 view of the West Pier shows it in its final form, with the central Concert Hall built in 1916.

71496

Another 1921 view of the West Pier showing clearly its completed buildings. Deckchairs are lined up on the Kings Road Promenade.

71486
This 1921 view taken from the pier, shows many changes since 1902; the Concert Hall, lifeboats and the fashions.

78309
This 1925 picture shows the boating lake. Between the wars, the pier was used for day trips to France, and had its own Custom's officials.

B208015
1920s view of the West Pier looking towards King's Road and the Metropole Hotel.

CHAPTER 2
THE SEAFRONT: ROTTINGDEAN TO THE PALACE PIER

The steep cliffed nature of Brighton's eastern seafront, from Rottingdean to the Palace Pier gives it quite a different flavour to the seafront to the west. The beach lies well below the main cliff top road and was originally the ladies' bathing beach. Ladies would enter the water from bathing machines licensed by Brighton Corporation. They cost 9*d* per half hour (6*d* for gentlemen). There were 150 ladies' machines and 100 gentlemen's in 1880. Mixed bathing was finally sanctioned by the corporation in 1901 - and then only from bathing machines. Seventy nine years later the world was changed indeed, with Brighton as the first, major resort to sanction a naturist beach - at Cliff bathing beach below Duke's Mound.

East Brighton's seafront architecture is of the highest standard. It developed eastwards from the Steine from the 1790s and reached Kemp Town in the 1850s, a succession of inspiring terraces and villas including Eastern Terrace and Royal Crescent as well as the fine Grade 1 listed Kemp Town estate itself. During the 'Fashionable Season' between October and January, the rich and famous would 'promenade' by the sea and on the pier in the mornings, and then spend the afternoon driving along the seafront drives of Marine Parade and King's Road from Kemp Town to Brunswick Town.

In order to protect the prestigious dwellings of Marine Parade, a great sea wall was built along the cliff in the 1830s and a road constructed along it. This was immediately fashionable with 'promenaders' because of its sheltered location and its proximity to the Chain Pier. It was rebuilt as Madeira Drive (known as Madeira Road until the First World War) and improved in the 1890s with the building of Madeira Terrace raised on its graceful cast iron arches, and the Madeira Lift which carried people from Madeira Drive to Marine Parade. Madeira Drive has always been popular for events like the National Speed Trials.

The Undercliff walk from Black Rock to Rottingdean opened in 1933, part of a scheme to protect the cliffed coast. The extension to Saltdean opened in 1935, at the same time as Rottingdean swimming pool, in its superb location at the foot of the cliffs. The open air pool at Black Rock opened in 1936. Both pools have now closed and the Undercliff at Black Rock is dominated by the Marina.

Other attractions of the eastern seafront included the Chain Pier of 1823, the Aquarium which opened in 1872, and Volk's Electric Railway, opened in 1883, the first such railway, which still runs along the shore between the beach and Madeira Drive.

R62082

A picture postcard view of Rottingdean seafront, looking west towards Brighton and Worthing in about 1965.

R62065

The Rottingdean sea water baths opened in 1935, and enjoyed a superb location beneath the cliffs. Shown here in the 1960s, they closed in 1990.

B208508
Black Rock swimming pool opened in 1936. This 1950s view shows how popular it became. Roedean school stands on the cliff above the present site of the Brighton Marina.

B208035
Black Rock swimming pool on a busy summer day in the 1950s. Behind is Marine Gate, a block of flats dating from the 1930's. The pool closed in 1978.

48517

A 1902 view looking westwards along Madeira Terrace towards the piers. Promenaders stroll in the sun and a horse drawn vehicle drives along Madeira Drive.

71499

A 1921 view looking westwards from Marine Parade, showing the handsome Regency seafront and buses parked along Madeira Drive.

B208070

A 1950s view from Duke's Mound. On the right, can be seen the 1890s Madeira Lift, which enabled prome-naders to take the easy way up to Marine Parade.

B208069

This is a 1950s view of the imposing Eastern Terrace, nine four-storeyed houses on Marine Parade which date from the 1820s.

B208503
A hot summer view taken in the 1950s. On the left is the Palace Pier entrance whilst on the right is the Aquarium and terrace.

B208071
A 1950s view taken from the top of the Aquarium sun terrace. Coaches are parked along Madeira Drive.

B208019

This 1950s view from close to the entrance to the Palace Pier, looks East along Marine Parade. Note the lack of road markings.

B208502

A 1950s view of the remodelled Aquarium, with its two square kiosk's and Pagoda roofs.

HIGH CLASS VAUDEVILLE
THIS WEEK
"FANTASY"
3·15 TWICE DAILY 7·30
EACH WEEK

OPEN 10 TILL 9·30 DAILY
ALLIGATOR HUNDREDS SPECIMENS
TERRAPIN 12 & 3

VAUDEVILLE

CIGARS

71498

The Aquarium Clock Tower and entrance in 1921. By the end of the decade, this frontage was swept away.

22238
This 1889 view shows the entrance to the Aquarium which opened in 1872. Goat carts awaiting customers are visible on the left of the picture.

B208504
Looking east along the front to the Aquarium and Marine Drive, here thronged with holiday makers, in the mid-1950s.

B208097
A bustling view of the promenade by the Aquarium entrance in the late 1950s. The occupants of the deckchairs are clearly enjoying their rest.

48515
An early 1900s view from the Palace Pier, looking to the West Pier. The Union Jack flutters proudly from one of the many hotels.

48514A
A 1902 view looking west from the Palace Pier. Bathing machines can be seen drawn up at the top of the beach.

48514
Another 1902 view looking west. Bathing machines vie for space with fishing boats on the 'gentlemen's beach'.

B208096
A 1950s view looking eastwards from the Palace Pier along the seafront to the cliffs at Rottingdean.

B208116
Looking west from Palace Pier in about 1955. Bathing machines and boats have vanished from the beach.

41890

A jostling 1898 view of Brighton Beach: holidaymakers, entertainers, boats and bathing machines fill the picture. The Palace Pier is still under construction.

R62084

A 1960s view of the Undercliff Walk and beach at Rottingdean, looking east along the cliffs towards Newhaven. The view is little changed today.

B208115

The handsome skyline presented by Brighton to the sea as seen from the Palace Pier in the 1950s.

CHAPTER 3
The Seafront: The Palace Pier to King's Esplanade

Busy, breezy 'Doctor Brighton', where the crowds came to 'take the waters' and be dipped in the sea, is epitomised by the pictures of the seafront from the Palace Pier westwards to Hove. King's Road, the seafront road of west Brighton, is named after George I who opened it in 1822. It was part of the principal 'carriage drive' of the town and as such was not surfaced with tarmac until 1910. It was widened in the 1850s and 60s and again in the 1880s, when the King's Road Arches were constructed beneath it and the birdcage bandstand built.

There is notable architecture in West Brighton, although the twentieth century has punctuated and interrupted the majestic sweep of Regency and Victorian buildings. Big hotels like The Grand, The Norfolk and The Metropole still face seaward, but modern developments have replaced the old Bedford and the famous Mutton's, which closed in 1929. Regency developments like Brunswick Terrace (Hove) and Regency Square lend their elegance to West Brighton.

The Lower Esplanade from Palace Pier westwards to the lawns of Hove has always been the 'honky tonk' part of Brighton's seafront, the haunt of stalls and entertainers and later of private beach chalets, cafes and amusement arcades. The Western Lawns beyond the bandstand were laid out in the 1880s and improved in 1925 with the addition of a boating pool and putting green, and again for the Festival of Britain in 1953.

Beach donkeys were a feature of the Brighton seafront until the Second World War. They plied the lower esplanade with their youthful mounts, since the pebbly beach made it impossible for them to be ridden there. Dark rumours hung around these donkeys in the mid nineteenth century, for they were reputed to be used clandestinely by the local smuggling fraternity to carry contraband spirits. Goat carts were available for children to hire from the 1830s - they were expensive, costing one shilling per hour by the mid nineteenth century. The beach was always busy, and beach entertainers, including 'minstrels' with blackened faces were very popular, though frequently of dubious merit. From 1891 pierrots, in their black and white costumes were introduced from France. During the nineteenth and early twentieth centuries there was a great vogue for boat trips from the beach and many former fishing vessels were thus employed, notably the *Skylark*, a boat that became so famous that *Skylark* became a generic term for the pleasure boats of Brighton.

48503

Another 1902 view shows a timeless scene; children playing on the seafront. Before the invention of deckchairs, the beach sported wooden benches.

48492
This Edwardian view of King's Road shows the famous Metropole and Grand Hotels as well as Bolla & Bucchi's Restaurant in the King's Road Arches on the Lower Esplanade.

71492

Nineteen years later, the big hotels gaze impassively on a less crowded beach, whilst the New Savoy Arches Restaurant is touting for business on the Lower Esplanade.

78308

Only a few years separates this from the previous scene, but there has been a further change of ownership of the arches, now reduced to selling ice cream.

48502
Nautical Brighton, 1902; a steamer arrives at the West Pier, whilst yachts are drawn up on the beach ready for sailing.

B208120
The centrepiece of this 1950s scene is the putting green on the Lower Esplanade, constructed in 1935-8. Cafes and amusements are found in the King's Road Arches.

B208118

The seafront in the 1950s looking to the West Pier. The ice cream men are out in force and a beer lorry delivers to a cafe.

48501

A 1902 view looking eastwards from the West Pier to the new Palace Pier. The big groynes were built to counter coastal erosion.

71490

A 1921 view of the parade. The deck chairs have today made way for a cycle track, and there is a paddling pool on the extreme left. The ramp is above the site of Brighton's lifeboat station, 1887-1931.

B208090

A busy and nostalgic scene of the paddling pool by the West Pier taken in the 1950's. The pool was constructed in 1935-8.

B208507

This evening view from the mid-1950s looks to the ramp from whence the previous picture was taken.

B208013

Another view of the paddling pool looking westwards. Note the private chalets under the arches.

B208123

A final view of the paddling pool, taken one morning in the 1950s. The rectangular entrance kiosk to the West Pier looks resplendent.

78312

This 1925 view of The Metropole shows little change since the beginning of the century. The massive proportions of this red brick hotel dwarf its more modest neighbours.

27609

This 1890 view shows two of Brighton's famous hotels, on the left, The Metropole, which opened that year, the largest hotel outside London, and on the right, The Grand.

71491

The classic 1920s view of Brighton. This evocative picture of the promenaders is reminiscent to one of the most famous Brighton posters of the interwar years, entitled *Brighton: Fame & Fashion.*

B208130

This 1950s view shows Hove's elegant seafront sandwiched between Portslade Power Station, on the far left, and the 1930s Embassy Court in the centre, the first 'modern' building to go up here.

B208088

A happy 1950s scene at the Children's boating pool first opened in 1925. The building beyond was built for the Festival of Britain as the Western Bathing Pavilion.

B208124

The boating pool was a favourite spot in the 1950s, and this photo suggests that it would continue forever. Sadly, it was not to be. It is now a Petanque terrain.

48505

A classic Edwardian scene: elegance, straw hats and parasols promenade along the King's Esplanade, a fashionable resort at the height of its fame.

27607

A timeless late Victorian scene along the King's Esplanade: in the foreground, mother and father are taking their girl for a stroll along the terrace.

B208091
Clock golf was played in the 1950s on the western side of the Western Bathing Pavilion.

33719
This 1894 view from the bandstand shows a donkey on the Lower Esplanade watched by a child up on the Parade. The old Bedford Hotel is in the centre of the picture.

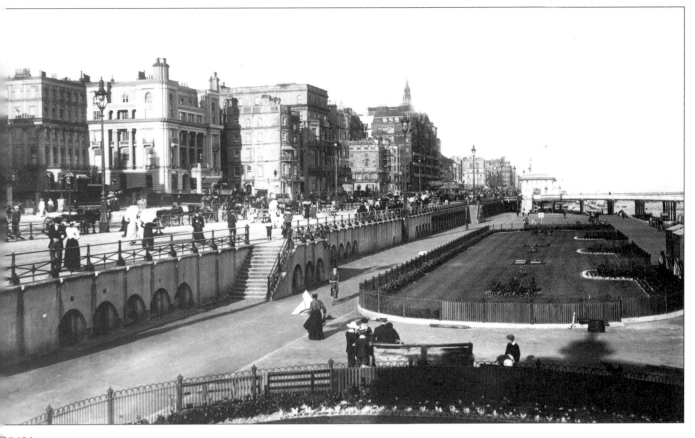

48491
Time moves on, but little has changed in this 1902 scene. Horse carriages are visible on King's Road whilst bathing machines are drawn up on the right.

71488
This 1921 view of the same spot shows some changes, with deckchairs ranged along the parade.

33721
This 1894 view is looking west from the bandstand to Hove. The low building on the right is the former Brunswick Baths, now replaced by Embassy Court.

71489
This 1921 view looks west to the Hove boundary and the Peace Memorial, actually a memorial to Edward VII.

78303

This 1925 view looking to the Peace Memorial proudly shows the newly created Brunswick Gardens, part of major improvements to the seafront.

B208506

A 1950s view looking from the Hove Boundary to the bandstand and showing the gardens more closely.

B208505
Looking east across Hove Lawns in about 1955. The Peace Memorial and the Norfolk Hotel dominate the Brighton-Hove boundary.

71500
This evocative view echoes the distinctive atmosphere of Hove – the elegant and sophisticated sister of Brighton. The superb Regency skyline provides a fitting setting for walking the baby.

71503

Courtenay Terrace is the only group of houses which had gardens backing onto the beach. The built-up prom today, extends westwards past the houses, but miraculously they and their gardens survive.

H128011

This gentle 1960s scene of Hove bowling green is a world away from bustling, cosmopolitan Brighton. The green is still very much part of the Hove scene.

H128006

The Hove boating lake in the mid-1960s was a venue for model boat enthusiasts. Today it is used for wind-surfing.

CHAPTER 4
BRIGHTON TOWN

Old Brighton was a coastal fishing village bounded by West Street, East Street and North Street, that area of town now known as 'the lanes'. There was once a South Street, and indeed a whole 'lower town' on the beach, but they were claimed by the sea in the early eighteenth century. To the east of East Street a marshy valley, the Steine (pronounced 'Steen') with a little stream, the Wellesbourne, ran down to the coast. Here fishermen would spread their nets to dry, and here was the farmhouse where the Prince Regent (George IV) stayed, took a liking to the place and ended up building the Royal Pavilion, Brighton's best known building, which is now listed Grade 1.

Brighton was a 'spa' town before the Prince arrived, thanks to the, *Treatise on the use of sea water* by Dr Russell of Lewes, published in 1754. Royal patronage ensured that it became the fashionable place to 'take the waters' and the town developed apace. Up went the Regency terraces, squares and villas for which Brighton is famous, a style of building which continued here well into the Victorian era. The Steine became the place to 'promenade' and various improvements took place with the building of the North and South Parades. In 1823 the Steine was enclosed with tall iron fencing and the following year it was provided with gas lights.

When the railway arrived in Brighton in 1841 it brought with it a new kind of visitor, the 'tripper' and the town grew greatly in size, filling up with hotels, boarding houses, cafes, restaurants and theatres. North Street and East Street, the principal shopping streets, bustled with activity. Brighton was also famed for its schools, which took advantage of Brighton's reputation as a health-giving place and which found perfect accommodation in large Regency villas.

Brighton's parish church, St Peter's, was built in the 1820s at Richmond Green, just north of the Steine, and designated as the parish church in 1873. It was originally a chapel-of-ease to the old parish church of St Nicholas, set up on the hill to the west and the burial place of Brighton worthies like Martha Gunn, the most famous Brighton 'dipper' and Phoebe Hessell, who had disguised herself as a man to fight in the British army alongside her lover. St Peter's was designed by Sir Charles Barry, later architect of the Houses of Parliament.

B2085012
A fascinating 1880s view across the Steine showing Marlborough House, Steine House and Blenheim House. All three buildings are still standing. The magnificent fountain was built in 1846 for Queen Victoria's 27th birthday.

22245
An 1889 view of the Pavilion. This former Royal Palace is Brighton's best known building, and is now a museum.

B208501

This 1950s view of North Street looks to the Countess Huntingdon's Chapel. Hugely popular in its day and seating 2,000 people, it was demolished in 1972.

48524

The Dome in 1902. It was originally built in 1803-8 as stables for the Pavilion, but was converted to a magnificent concert hall, capable of seating 2,500 people.

22244

Another superb 1889 view of Pavilion showing clearly its remarkable Indian façade built for the Prince of Wales (George IV) in the early 1800s.

B208081

This 1950s view of the Pavilion shows off its ornate oriental style to advantage. A Grade 1 listed building, it has been restored in recent years to its original condition.

B208079

A further 1950s view of the Pavilion. Queen Victoria found it not to her taste, and sold the redundant palace to Brighton Corporation for £50,000.

B208018

This view, taken in the 1950s, shows the main entrance to the Pavilion. It is difficult to imagine how it must have appeared to Brighton's simple fisherfolk.

41901

Although Queen Victoria deserted Brighton for the Isle of Wight, the town celebrated her Diamond Jubilee by opening the Victoria Gardens. This splendid statue forms the centrepiece.

48523

St Peter's, the parish church of Brighton, dominates the area just north of the Steine. It was built in 1824-8. Today, it is rather marooned between the London and Lewes roads.

B2085015

A steam driven engine and what appears to be a furrowing machine, standing in London Road in about 1900. It is probably engaged in ripping up the roads to construct the tramways.

48522

The Steine in 1902. Note the tall railings and the lack of traffic. The trams began operating the year before, with the Steine as their main terminus.

B2085008

A wartime view of the 75 ft high clock tower, built in 1888 to celebrate the Queens Golden Jubilee a year earlier.

B2085002

A turn of the century view of the tramway construction taking place in the Steine. The photographer is looking towards North Road.

B2085010

Another fine shot of the tramway construction in the Steine, looking directly to where the previous photograph was taken. The extensive network was completed in 1904, and trams ran until just before the Second World War.

B2085004

An excellent close-up of the navvies building the tramlines round the Steine. The photographer has caught to perfection the hard labour required.

B2085001
Tramway construction at the junction of Lewes Road and Elm Grove. The tracks curving away to the right terminated by the racecourse. This view has changed greatly today.

29359
Built in 1854 as the Diocesian Training College for schoolmistresses, this flint building was taken over by the Royal Engineers and is now the Brighton Business Centre.

B2085007

This 1902 view shows tram No.22 heading down Queen's Road from the Station. The buildings behind have all been demolished and replaced.

27756

Brighton Corporation acquired 67 acres of meadow at Preston Manor in 1883, and the park was opened the following year. This view was taken in 1890.

CHAPTER 5
ENVIRONS OF BRIGHTON

Since the early nineteenth century Brighton has been synonymous with fame and fashion, so, perhaps, it is only natural, that nearby Hove prides itself on its gentility. Hove has grown from a number of hamlets to the west of Brighton. It has ancient roots but only started to grow in the nineteenth century when it began to fall into the gravitational pull of its big sister. The waters of St Anne's Well, a chalybeate spring were recommended by Dr Russell in his treatise and brought visitors to Hove. Brunswick Terrace, perhaps the most magnificent Regency development in Britain, was completed in 1830, and further seafront terraces and squares followed. It says much that, when you stand on the beach near the West Pier, the Hove seafront stands out as totally unspoilt, and little changed from these pictures.

Beyond the seafront, Church Street is Hove's main commercial street. Up until 1966, it was dominated by the old Hove Town Hall. Although this has now gone, Church Street retains a discreet and gentle air. Hove has some particularly fine churches. The old parish church of St Andrew's nestles incongruously under the Victorian gasometer, and dates back to medieval times. All Saints, built at the end of the nineteenth century, is a superbly grand affair. St Leonard's, Aldrington, went up in the 1870s, and St John the Baptist's, which was built in 1852 to serve the Adelaide Crescent development, adds a elegance with a soaring spire of about 1870.

To the east of Brighton is Rottingdean, a coastal village sheltering in a little combe, and still largely untroubled by the presence of its noisy neighbour. If Hove is Brighton's genteel suburb, Rottingdean is Brighton's country cousin. Since the growth of Brighton, Rottingdean, with its twelfth century church built on Saxon foundations, and its tranquil village pond, has long been a magnet for artists and authors. During the Victorian era many were drawn to its peace and solitude, almost cheek by jowl with Brighton. The most famous were Rudyard Kipling and Sir Edward Burne-Jones. Their houses still stand.

Behind Brighton to the north, rise the smooth, rolling South Downs. It was inevitable that Brighton's visitors would turn inland and discover their beauty. The magnet was the Devil's Dyke, one of the highest points on the Downs, which has magnificent views over the Weald. A branch railway put the Dyke on the map, and other strange contraptions, a hair-raising cable car across the Dyke and a funicular railway down the scarp slope of the Downs, added to its attractions. All have long since closed.

R62044

A mid-1950s view of Rottingdean windmill. It was built in 1802, fell into disuse later in the century and was later restored.

R62043

The secluded nature of Rottingdean is evident in this 1960s view, showing it tucked into a fold of the South Downs.

R62081

Rottingdean pond in the 1960s. It was once popular with downland shepherds, but it dried up in 1976, and is now pumped from the well.

R62059

Another 1960s view of Rottingdean pond, looking round to the war memorial, a simple obelisk erected in 1920. Today, the roads are considerably busier.

37139

A1896 view of the village, Rottingdean. The village looks threadbare by comparison with its manicured look today, reflecting its steady gentrification.

37140

A 1896 view of The Street, Rottingdean. The photographer has the undivided attention of a group of children.

R62087

This picture, taken in the mid-1960s, is taken from a similar position to the previous picture. The roofline has changed little, but shops now front the street, which is busy with cars.

R62075

This 1960s view shows the road linking the cliffs and shore with the coast road. Thirty years or so later, this view is little altered.

R62089

A view of The Street, looking south, in the mid 1960s. Again, the view has not changed substantially in the past 30 years, but the road has become busier.

37143

Many schools were established in the Brighton area, the bracing air being ideal for children. Perhaps the most famous is Roedean, established in new buildings on the clifftop a few years after this picture was taken in 1896.

22255

An 1889 picture of St Margaret's Church, Rottingdean. The church dates from the twelfth century but stands on the site of a Saxon church.

R62048

St Margaret's church in the 1960s. The church is pleasantly situated by the green, the lychgate being added in 1897.

R62078

A 1960s view of Rottingdean village. Part of these cottages date back to Tudor times, but otherwise they are a 1930s redevelopment.

R62020

Tudor Close House was a skillful 1920s conversion of much older farm buildings into seven houses. They were converted into a hotel, as seen in this 1950s view, but shortly afterwards was reconverted back to twenty-nine flats.

R62061

The Rottingdean house of the painter Edward Burne-Jones, seen in about 1960. Burne-Jones lived here from 1880 to his death in 1898. The house was once three separate houses.

B208048

This wonderful 1950s view shows Brighton's municipal camping ground, the first in the country, which was opened in May 1938.

B208058

Another view of the camping ground, showing the former farm buildings on the left. The racecourse on the top of the hill show just how close the camping ground was to Brighton.

B208511

The camping ground was situated in the Sheepcote valley, between the racecourse and Black Rock. It incorporated the former Newhouse Farm. It closed in the early 1990s.

48507

A 1902 view of Hove's Victoria Statue at the south end of Grand Avenue, at one time the most prestigious street in Hove.

H128003

A mid-1950s view of Brittany Road. Situated just of Kingsway, the road is not changed greatly today, although there are many more cars.

H128002

A similar view to the previous picture, but showing Kingsway and the parade of shops. Little has changed today, although the Post Office sign on the side of Brown's shop has disappeared.

41895

A splendid 1898 view of The Drive, Hove. The view is substantially the same today, although the trees have grown considerably.

41896

A bustling scene in Church Road, Hove, in 1898. This view is dominated by the old Town Hall. In the background can be seen the gasometer.

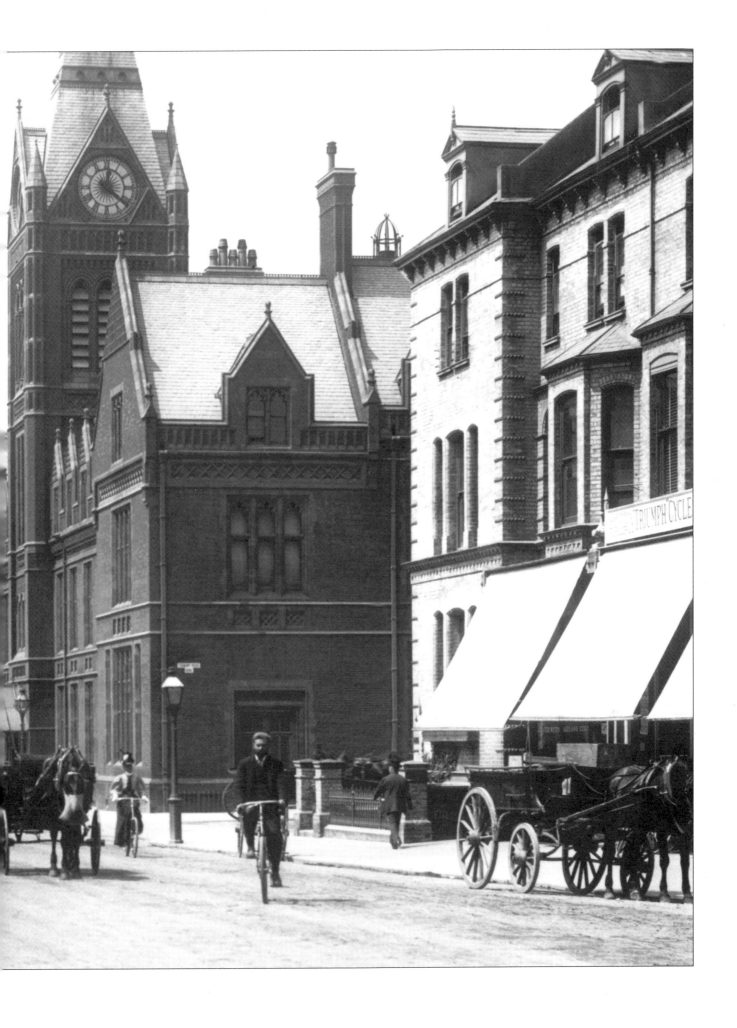

H128005
Looking eastwards down Kingsway in the mid-1950s. Again, this view has not changed greatly, the pub is still open for trade, although the road has acquired traffic islands.

H128004
Derek Avenue, Hove, in the 1950s. Today, the trees have matured, and the road is now lined with cars.

1894

A close up of the handsome Town Hall. In this 1898 view, the Hall was only 16 years old. Sadly, it was ravaged by fire in the 1960s and demolished.

H128010

Further west along Church Street is St Andrew's, the old parish church of Hove. As in this 1960s view, the church is today overshadowed by the town gasometer.

R62037
Rottingdean windmill in the mid-1960s. Legend has it, that this famous smock mill was used by smugglers for signalling.

41897
An 1898 study of St John-the-Baptist, Palmeira Square, Hove. This elegant church was built in 1852 to serve the Adelaide Crescent development.

H128008
Another 1960s study of one of Hove's excellent churches, this time St Leonard's. The church, and its lychgate, are little changed today.

41898
A 1898 view of Hove's congregational church, situated at the top of Ventnor Villas.

33765

An 1894 view from the top of Devil's Dyke, looking north to the Weald. The church and village of Poynings are in the foreground.

33764

A view of the deep Devil's Dyke valley in 1894. The old Roman road to Portslade can be seen climbing the side in the foreground. Because sheep no longer graze the downs, the Dyke today is covered in vegetation.

48527

A 1902 view looking directly to the Dyke. To the left of the flagpole can be seen a pier of the Dyke cable car, which stretched across the valley. This vertigo-inducing ride lasted from 1894 to 1907. The places where the piers stood are still visible.

B208509

A mid-1950s view of the road over the downs from Poynings to Brighton, with the road to the left heading up to Devil's Dyke. At the bottom of the road is the hamlet of Saddlescombe, now owned by the National Trust.

Pictorial Memories Collection

A great new range of publications featuring the work of innovative Victorian photographer Francis Frith.

FRITH PUBLISHING, WATERTON ESTATE, BRIDGEND,
GLAMORGAN, CF31 3XP.

TEL: 01656 668836   FAX: 01656 668710

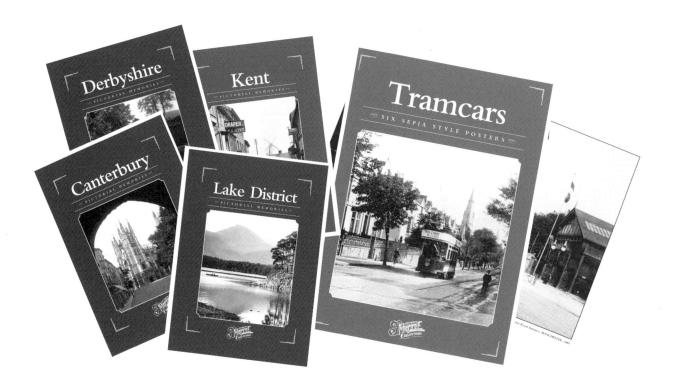

Themed Poster Books £4.99

000-7	Canals and Waterways	
001-5	High Days and Holidays	
003-1	Lakes and Rivers	
004-x	Piers	
005-8	Railways	
044-9	Ships	
002-3	Stone Circles & Ancient Monuments	
007-4	Tramcars	

Town & City Series £9.99

010-4	Brighton & Hove	
015-5	Canterbury	
012-0	Glasgow & Clydeside	
011-2	Manchester	
040-6	York	

Town & City series Poster Books £5.99

018-x	Around Brighton	
023-6	Canterbury	
043-0	Derby	
020-1	Glasgow	
011-2	Manchester	
041-4	York	

County Series £9.99

024-4	Derbyshire	
028-7	Kent	
029-5	Lake District	
031-7	Leicestershire	
026-0	London	
027-9	Norfolk	
030-9	Sussex	
025-2	Yorkshire	

County Series Poster Books £4.99

032-5	Derbyshire	
036-8	Kent	
037-6	Lake District	
039-2	Leicestershire	
034-1	London	
035-x	Norfolk	
038-4	Sussex	
033-3	Yorkshire	

Available soon

County Series £9.99

045-7	Berkshire	
053-8	Buckinghamshire	
055-4	East Anglia	
077-5	Greater London	
051-1	Lancashire	
047-3	Staffordshire	
049-x	Warwickshire	
063-5	West Yorkshire	

County Series Poster Books £4.99

046-5	Berkshire	
054-6	Buckinghamshire	
056-2	East Anglia	
078-3	Greater London	
052-x	Lancashire	
048-1	Staffordshire	
050-3	Warwickshire	
064-3	West Yorkshire	

Country Series £9.99

075-9	Ireland	
071-6	North Wales	
069-4	South Wales	
073-2	Scotland	

Country Series Poster Books £4.99

076-7	Ireland	
072-4	North Wales	
070-8	South Wales	
074-0	Scotland	

A selection of our 1999 programme:
County Series and Poster Books
Devon, Cornwall, Essex,
Nottinghamshire, Cheshire.

Town and City Series and Poster Books
Bradford, Edinburgh, Liverpool, Nottingham,
Stamford, Bristol, Dublin,
Stratford-upon-Avon, Bath, Lincoln,
Cambridge, Oxford, Matlock, Norwich.

Themed Poster Books
Castles, Fishing, Cricket, Bridges, Cinemas,
The Military, Cars.